if you need me
you can always
find me
laughing under
the rain

Laughing Under the Rain

Laughing Under
the Rain

Collected Poems

C. Churchill

C. Churchill

Laughing Under the Rain

other books available by C. Churchill
Petals of the Moon
Wildflower Tea
Ravens Moon
Mirror Mirror
Chasing Pines
Racing Ravens
Screaming into the Forest

on social media @cc_writes

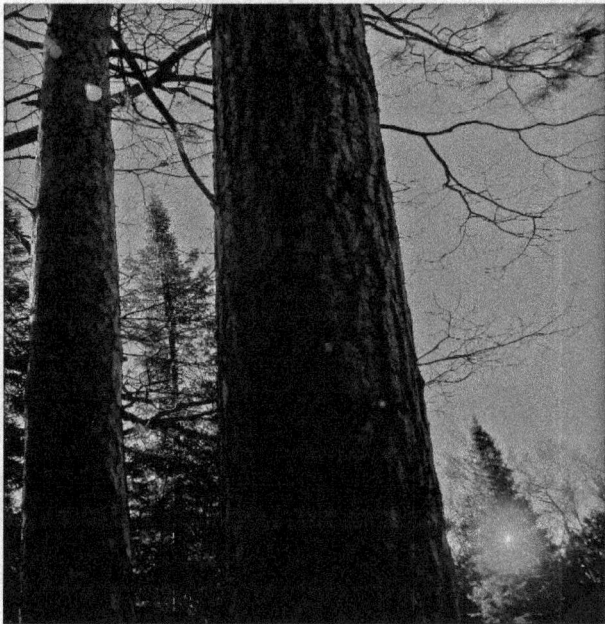
Start here

maybe it's time
we all look in the mirror
and see the h e r o

Screaming into the forest
laughing under the rain
trying everything we can
to beat this place

the place of breaking
the place of pain
where we were left on the edge
under the rain

we have all been there
in one way or another
screaming into a void
running for cover

a breath we take
our lungs now full
our belly laughs
and the rains come to still

-laughing under the rain

My feet are bricks
the ground it shakes
what once were feathers
have been replaced

every mountain, every valley
every path less chosen
has calloused these feet
till emboldened

I have solid footing
my steps are true
and these bricks seem weightless
in my journey to you

-solid

sweet surrender

I'm not running away
I'm breathing
without an
a u d i e n c e

in a corner
paint peels
fingernails short
from repeated fails
nubs of charcoal
smudge kohl
blending tears
and prints
of hands worn
wear in melancholy
a corner I sit
as the paint peels
and I can't seem to move
as time fades in and out
the sun travels the day in shadows
and my hands move across
this portrait
a portrait I have been smearing
with sadness instead of hope
all the while
it should be capturing the sun
not the shadows
and the paint peels

-in this corner

C. Churchill

I hear the ocean in you
a depth I had never knew
I collect memories in you
a hollow to be filled
this shell another home
I fill with sand and old bones
a skeleton collects
among this debris of memory
a tear
a smile
a shell
discarded
a home no longer there
no longer invited
just a quick toss
and goodbye
in the waves of your ocean
a collector I remain
always moving forward

-oceans

wild beauty

sunlight only illuminates

the need for a thirst to be

q u e n c h e d

old wooden beams
warm and warped
held together by
sunshine and strings
a dream of what was
and a sting of what is
pass over these timbers
a home
a shelter
a bending bough
where we find comfort
in what is now
safety in the known
even though it is warped
a place we call home
when what it truly is
is hope

-safety

C. Churchill

on a roadside summer
we count the cars
where they come from
where they go
we don't really care
that is too much to grasp
why and where
on a roadside summer
we haven't the time
only to count them
here then gone
as summers pass
the cars they change
but passing time
remains the same
on a roadside summer
here then gone

-counting cars

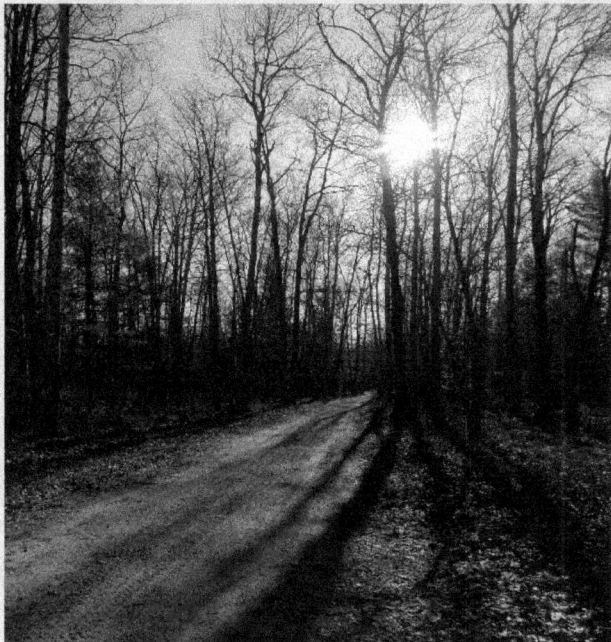

long days shadow

I collect journeys
in my pocket
like lint from the dryer
not worth much to anyone else
but it some way
they always make me
s m i l e

I pass the lily
the swamp
the pond
checking the light
by the heat on my cheek
eyes closed
letting my feet take charge
shadows cast on lids
letting me know to pause
not to stop
just be cautious
the darkness can be dangerous
if you decide to run through
but if you pause
and explore
you may find comfort
in the unknown
instead of running through your own shadow
try to find comfort in the stroll

-comfort

C. Churchill

ankle deep
embrace the chill
one step forward
trying for numb

feel the current
lace my thighs
cramp my belly
in forgotten lies

not time to go under
not just yet
the chill is still there
waiting for numb

currents now sweeping
my breasts, my shoulders
my heart there, there it is
there is the numb

time to go under
look from below
swimming in blackwater
far from the sky

I float
this is mine
this river
fully submerged

mine
my river
my time
my numbness

a break, the sun
the chill returns
but it's in diamonds
spread across my eyes

and my river
in all its glory
is a treasure
whether numb or chilled

-river

C. Churchill

from trunk to bloom
a journey past youth
but the young still come
and continue this truth

at branches coil
new growth begins
arms stretch the spoil
in awe and whim

from elder to innocent
and whore to root
we all ride branches
wild and confused

where we land,
who's to say
a leaf, a dream
only a breeze away

-branches

to be weightless

flying or
falling
off this edge
I am unsure
but I swallow
and leap
with every
f i b e r
of my being

I assure you
there is no shame
in being a fool
for love
for life
for dreams
for you
for them
dance, trip, scream, love
foolishly
till the end

-a fool

C. Churchill

my love lay broken
at the edge of the bed
a receipt
to remind me
at years end
that what we spend
may indeed
put us in debt
but it was worth wine and roses
when we first met

- receipt

make the time

there are only moments
and memories
stop watching the clock
and open your
e y e s

fill the kettle
add some heat
wait for the whistle
break these tired feet
soon it will be time
the thoughts to steam away
in chipped porcelain
promises in the fray
a smile to come
a sigh, a breath
tired feet
taking a much-needed rest

- *kettle*

C. Churchill

a grain here
a grain there
shotgun shell
an intent stare
deafness echoes
between these years
blinding explosion
quelling these fears
the target hit
as predicted
and my hands
kissed powder
once restricted

- *powder*

when we spin

if only
collecting flags
created capes
instead of
c a r n i v a l s

I want to see the circus
instead of be the circus
where lions roar
and zebras prance
where I can unsee the evil
and just laugh and dance

I want to see the circus
instead of bleed the circus
where carnival colors stripe walls
and bellies bellow
where clowns are not scary
and chaos is calming

I want to see the circus
instead of breathe the circus
with a full heart
and reckless laughter
where I can unsee
what has become of me

- *circus*

C. Churchill

my walls are six feet thick
and crystal clear
begging passerby's
to gather near
exposed and vulnerable
was how it began
and now a sideshow
without a plan
a boardwalk to nowhere
an abandoned feast
an aquarium of oddities
to say the least
but here I rest
glazed behind walls
that are six feet thick
hoping to stay small

- *aquarium*

a taste of truth

cherries ripe
on branches sway
ready to strip
a stem today
sour in your hand
before the morrow
better now before the
f a l l o w

my eyes flutter
at a sliver of sunlight
peeking on me
through curtains
not quite straight
a burn to my eyes
coated in last night's shadow
foggy to strain, focus
my arm stretch feels
a pillow bare
sloppy yawns of
broken breath
escape my tired frame
as I inhale, smelling coffee
and my dreary eyes lock on you
standing in the edge of my fantasy
with two cups of coffee
mumbling through a smile
something about
sugar or milk?

- *milk*

C. Churchill

fruit so full
juicy and soft
plucked fresh this mourn

to your delight
sunshine under skin
at your candor

nothing to hide
a wholly experience
explodes in mouths

plucked this morn
a fruit falls ripe
breakfast of champions

- peaches

skinny dip

we all learn
to swim
once we find
the
h o o k

in the deep end
of a drought
drowning
without a drop of water in sight

my skin is cracked
from the hot winds
my eyes no longer tear
for that well has run dry

yet I see the ripples of this mirage
begging me to drink
begging me to swim
begging me to cry

I am sinking in the deep end of a pool
with no water
with no lifeguard
with no ladder

with no escape
for this thirst
I will drown
as I try to drink

- pools

C. Churchill

we twist these words
until they lose truth
a mangled love
has come to roost

the sunrise is black
and the coffee is bitter
we have managed to create
this mangled critter

half beast
half rage, half stranger
takes place
reality hits a different way

when love is twisted
and the sunrise is black
this type of love
always falls off track

- mangled

melt with you

I don't mind if you are stubborn
I don't mind if you have fire
as long as
we burn together
to stay
w a r m

coffee hot
sun peeking
wondrous souls
no longer sleeping
hold tight
this cup of more
it is meant for
those who wonder
and live to explore

- *more*

a muse is a muse
and lust is lust

but when you must choose
love or the other

I hope you know it's the little things
that conquer

running straight into the fire
naked and free

having them catch you
just to see

if you will burn brighter
by their side

and keep the nights warm
together you ride

this life is meant for two
but only if you choose

love not the other

- *choices*

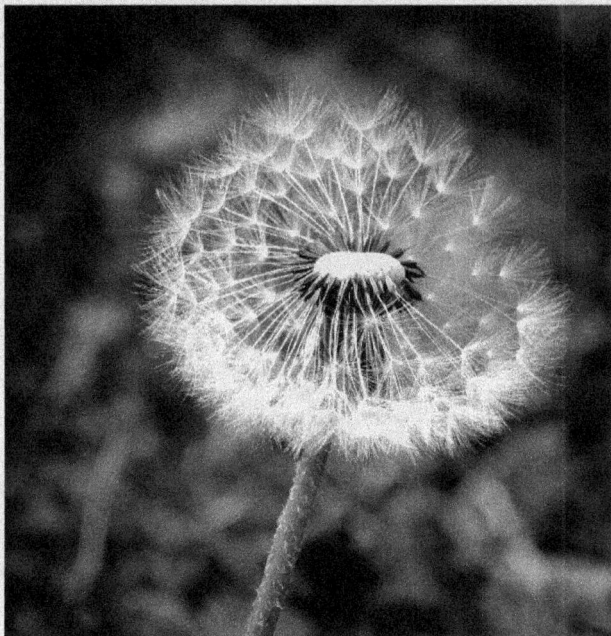

magic or wishes?

if it feels
like
m a g i c
chances are
it is

he was full of
terrible jokes
and burnt toast

but I laughed
and filled
my belly

with a smirk
he told me he loved me
and with smile he showed he cared

I never needed anything more
than someone who showed me
how to love

- how

A stop, I breathe
A gasp, I stop
A hand to lead
A fingertip to graze
A heart to bleed
but ready to play
I hear pins drop
I am ready to shudder
over moons and stars
I become the lover
a dream, I grasp
a moment, I stutter
for memories flood
of broken others
they need to flee
these cold feet
so, my sky
can open wide
so, I can see
truth over lies

- moons and stars

leave the light on

don't forget
to live
outside
the
f r a m e

mix, pour, cure, crack
handprints of babies
footprints of hearsay
initials of lovers
hearts to break
a cast of time
of life entombed
on this concrete
square right angle ruled
a segment, a piece
a permanence true
as chalk dust settles
in cracks of ruin
life springs forth
repeating a cycle
mix, pour, cure, crack
a concrete slab
a life taken back

- *concrete*

C. Churchill

elbows on tables
hands, covering smiles
laughing blindly
all the while

oven timers missed
the cup overflows
for the second or is it
the third time

between the candlelight
and the fridge light
a glow of perfection
arises in we

as hands
allow smiles
and elbows move
in sync

to press lips and hips
to countertops
and manners turn
to suggestions

blushing rises
from cups
overflowing
and countertops

if only they could speak but shh
allow the glow to rise
it spreads over flesh
a fresh nightlight

the oven timers sync
knees become weak
and there is no escape
this perfect heat

- countertops

one more word
one more line
one more verse
make it shine

a period, a question
an exclamation point
punctuation, please
this is a poetry joint

here we sling free
words that appease
not your normal list
hailed by grammar queens

yes, yes I agree
there is a time and place
but not on this page
and not at this pace

- poetry

sweet grass, sweet ass

tell me you love me
a thousand times
and always one more
so, my mind will let
my heart believe
y o u

I lay in wait
water full, warm
bubbles caress
fragrance the norm

becoming you here
a breath I bate
A sigh in turn
you I fate

this is to be
my greatest moon
the one where you say forever
and I say soon

where waters bead back
and slip into kisses
where we start forever
while firing near misses

where we clumsily
slip into fools
that know only blushing
and none of the rules

- *rules*

C. Churchill

let's skip rocks
over numbered paths
hop on one foot
then the other
till we fall in laugh
let's clink glasses
to watch others kiss
knowing full well
the joy and the bliss
let's carve initials
into old oak trees
and steal fresh roses
from old aunties
let's wet our shoulders
on nights that are hard
never forgetting to have each other
when we fall
let's share ice cream and loud screams
let's be married
without paper
without lease
without anything
besides belief

- married

a collector

whisper words
to fill this cup
so, I don't go thirsty
for
e a v e s d r o p s

under shadows cast
and butterfly's wing
a sneaky sunshine
a wrong turn into me
I caught you hard
no escape with a frown
time was lost, worth the while
lips became feet
and flesh a minefield
starting exploration explosion
across this windfall
from skinned knees to smile
a bomber skilled
to start this war
we shall both be killed
between hearts and minds
and back again
an ambush of delight
waiting to sin
under shadows cast
and butterfly's wing
starting and ending
with a wrong turn into me

- *bomber*

C. Churchill

with shiny locks
and rusty chains
the keeper
still keeps this cage

with every betrayal
new locks appear
on rusty will
landing tears

lies are branded
in a holding cell
a life in solitary
known as hell

where trust is fantasy
new locks appear
on rusty chains
I hold dear

- *cages*

privacy

circle the days
count the weeks
the months
the years
how long since
how long till next
how hard it is
to have patience
when your calendar
has been
e r a s e d

were you a liability, or was I?
with keys left in doors
and more tears cried
naked bruising in pleasure
then pain
all wild, all loud
with no refrain
the loudest love
I had ever known
we screamed in force
and through locked doors
wrong in every sense I suppose
but we loved, we cried
we let blood boil
into the sunrise
never wondering if we were wrong
just full force in this throng
at the end of the day
we were not well
but it was worth
this ticket to hell

- liability

stand, sit, kneel, pray
who loves you at the end of the day?
is it your weekly confession
that keeps you clean
or is it the person
that brings you to your knees
scared of your own shadow
doing as they please
you have decided to
waive your pleas
doing your time
hoping judgment doesn't frown
but all the while seeking
satisfaction beyond
stand, sit, kneel, pray
you are the priest
and there are demons to slay

- priest

ghosts

we tasted the fog
after the darkness
what a bitter sweet
a w a k e n i n g

running my hand
over boards
aged and weathered
quick stop

nail exposed
rusted through
from the rain
past the pause

a valley, a ridge
smooth and uneven
in cloud taking comfort
knowing this exists

storm after storm
but it is strong
even after the hurricane
built with purpose

to expand and contract
but still stand
its bigger than I even knew
as my hands make this journey

over the boards
the rain, the nails, the hurricane
the strength
the pain

- pain

C. Churchill

drag me sober
across the floor
tell me to whimper
at commands you adore

shock me, steal me
treat me so
what is this hell
when the wrong winds blow

shut my face
behind doors closed
watch me weather
below your storm

all the power you
think you posses
is hiding so close to reality
but three steps to the left

yes I scream
yes I cry
and I will no longer bleed
when I die

but yours I am not
not even a little
because hell or high water
will you get my wither

for reality is here
only a few steps away
and I have leapt
to save my stay

- bleed

C. Churchill

I am missing pieces
some black, some white
some days, some nights
a puzzle wrapped
in banality
not to be figured out
just accepted as
incomplete
because as sure
as one piece is found
I realize
yet another
is missing

- missing

skin

it always starts
with lust and trauma
anyone who says different
is selling
s o m e t h i n g

dress me in layers
keep me from the chill
left in the shadows
crepe skin starts to peel
roots coming
from all directions
layers break to light
improper selection
sweetness among fissures
a layer away
from redemption
peel me softly
paying attention
watch for the roots
the breaking skin
layer by layer
sweetness will win

- onion

C. Churchill

I heard something new
about myself today
at first, I laughed
for whom are they to say

I keep myself hidden
a mysterious coil
if they only knew
this blood doesn't boil

I have seen the tides
how rumors fly
how those who despise
end up in others lies

I don't challenge the rumor
I let it slide
for I am a mysterious coil
that does not oblige

- *rumor*

perspectives

we may not have wings
but that doesn't mean
we can't learn to
f l y

I want to read books
that set fire to my lips
I want to make art
that is wet with indiscretion
I want to not only survive
outside the box
but thrive
I want the freedom to choose
what makes me dream, makes me scream
and I want it to be in every color
especially the ones
that are
forbidden

- forbidden

C. Churchill

even though
I cross this plane barefoot
I don't mind the shards
placed under these feet
for the souls
that came before me
broke ceilings
impossible to meet
as shall I

- *barefoot*

foundations

it doesn't matter how we crumble
it doesn't matter if we fall
what matters
is how we
r e b u i l d

A window leaks
down the wall
a ravine assembles
in the fall

this stream has current
running along a shelf
making rivulets in the dust
a hundred years felt

muddy memories
spoil photographs
turning streams into
what ifs

-shelf

C. Churchill

prick my finger
tell me something real
my eyes try to see through
they try to feel
but the eye isn't clear
and the scissors are misplaced
and the shakiness of age
isn't winning this race
prick my finger
tell me something still
in the midst of the chaos
I have forgotten to feel
whip a stitch up
the side of an open heart
watch it beat
bring it to life
tear the fabric at the frayed edge
make it straight
make a pledge
prick my finger
show me something real
amidst the chaos
so I remember how to feel

- needle

almost there

when my journey
comes to pass
I hope I can answer
with a hell yes
a dash of pain
mixed with many dreams
and a love so strong
it brought me to my
k n e e s

like moths to a flame
fireflies dance
to the beat of my heart
lighting up a trance

with a magic
so high
that wonder is sprinkled
in the sky

as if the stars
were meant for dreamers
and the night meant
believers

- *stars*

C. Churchill

.

where do we go
when our heart needs to soar
when the sky rips open wide
and we forget to want more

where do we go
when the rules suddenly change
when love disappears
and turns to rage

where do we go
when home slips away
and tears fill voids
every god damn day

I will tell you a secret
one I recently discovered
there are no rules
when the sky is home to all beloved

- *limitless*

rewind

take the time
embrace the moments
even for a second
to become
b r e a t h l e s s

my heart has seen
a thousand tides
stuck in mud so deep
I closed my eyes
I opened them
to the sun
only to be blind
I began to run
following heart
into shadow
racing beats
wade through fallow
still, I chase
this blinding light
surviving on
my second sight

- second sight

It took me awhile
to see the stars
my eyes adjusting
to your sky

at first
all I saw was black
then little
by little

trust settled
in our eyes
it settled
in our universe

- together

enjoy the ride

Laughing Under
the Rain

even if it scares you
take the chance
give that dream a second
g l a n c e

C. Churchill

About the Author

C. Churchill maintains a residence in Northern Michigan
where she enjoys using nature as her muse for her writings
and photography. She has created a following on
social media that has launched several bestselling
poetry collections. This being her eleventh book of poetry
she is committed to her readers globally. Having a master's
degree in education she also finds time to help local students
with fulfilling their dreams in art and writing.

other books by C. Churchill

I am a Woman not a Winston
Color Body Feels
Wildflower Tea
Petals of the Moon
Racing Ravens
Chasing Pines
Mirror Mirror
Ravens Moon
- ish
Screaming into the Forest

C. Churchill can be found on social media @cc_writes

all dreamers welcome

C. Churchill